PRESSED FLOWERS

A Creative Guide

*This book is dedicated
to my daughter Gail*

PRESSED FLOWERS

A Creative Guide

CATHY BUSSI

Illustrations by Nicci Page

Photographs by Herman Potgieter

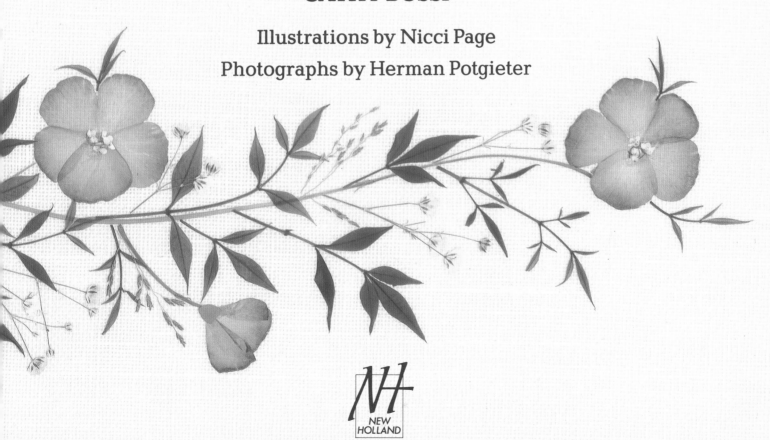

NH

NEW
HOLLAND

First published in the UK in 1988 by
New Holland (Publishers) Ltd
37 Connaught Street, London W2 2AZ
Second impression 1989

ISBN 1-85368 010 9

Editor: Michelé Ridgard
Designer: Janice Evans

Typeset by Diatype Setting
Reproduction by Photo Sepro
Printed and bound by CTP Book Printers

Contents

CRB.

In this natural design I used petals of the white floribunda rose 'Iceberg' for the flowers and rose leaves for the foliage. The colour change of the petals is clear.

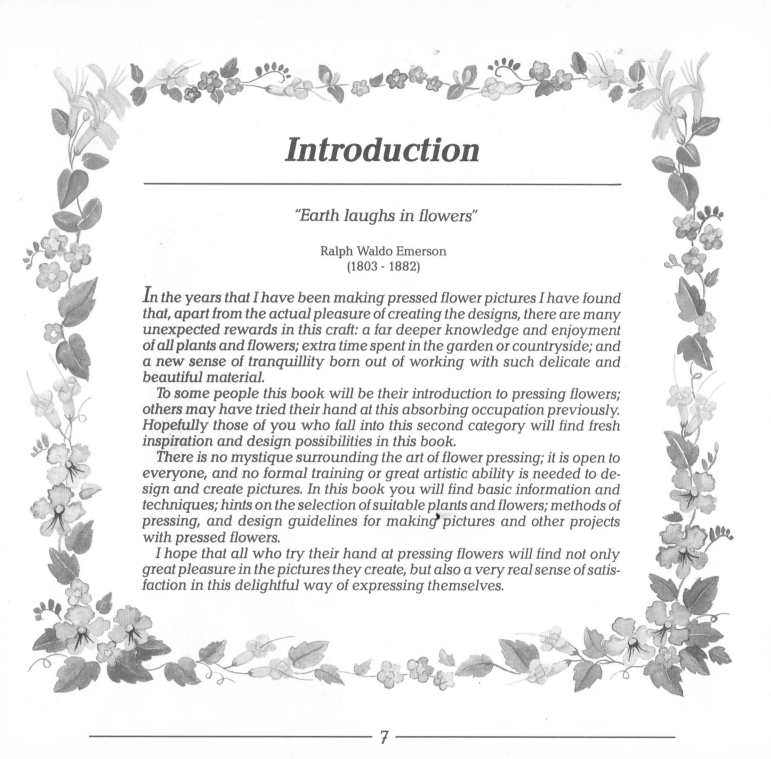

Introduction

"Earth laughs in flowers"

Ralph Waldo Emerson
(1803 - 1882)

In the years that I have been making pressed flower pictures I have found that, apart from the actual pleasure of creating the designs, there are many unexpected rewards in this craft: a far deeper knowledge and enjoyment of all plants and flowers; extra time spent in the garden or countryside; and a new sense of tranquillity born out of working with such delicate and beautiful material.

To some people this book will be their introduction to pressing flowers; others may have tried their hand at this absorbing occupation previously. Hopefully those of you who fall into this second category will find fresh inspiration and design possibilities in this book.

There is no mystique surrounding the art of flower pressing; it is open to everyone, and no formal training or great artistic ability is needed to design and create pictures. In this book you will find basic information and techniques; hints on the selection of suitable plants and flowers; methods of pressing, and design guidelines for making pictures and other projects with pressed flowers.

I hope that all who try their hand at pressing flowers will find not only great pleasure in the pictures they create, but also a very real sense of satisfaction in this delightful way of expressing themselves.

CHAPTER 1

Making a Start

Setting out on a new venture is both exciting and challenging. In the case of pressed flowers I think it is true to say that, once you take the first steps, you soon become deeply involved in this rewarding form of floral art. There is always something new to discover, and the natural beauty of the plants and flowers will inspire you to keep creating new designs. With very simple equipment, a love of plants and neat fingers you will be able to preserve the beauty of the flowers – not only in your pictures but also in a wide range of delightful gifts.

MATERIALS AND EQUIPMENT

One of the great advantages of pressing flowers is that the equipment you need is either simple to make or easy and inexpensive to buy. The most essential requirement, plant material, can be said to be a gift from nature, and it is given in such abundance that it often becomes difficult to know what to choose. Even if you only have a tiny garden, or are a flat-dweller with no garden at all, you will be able to choose from the wide variety of wild flowers, grasses and leaves to be found on a walk in the country, or simply growing at the side of the road.

The only other items you need when you start off are a flower press and several sheets of blotting paper and plain cardboard. It is not at all difficult to make a simple, yet most efficient, flower press and the other items are easily obtainable at reasonable prices.

BLOTTING PAPER

You require a good supply of blotting paper, and I suggest you cut and fold it as soon as you have purchased it. It is important to have several prepared sheets on hand at all times, as you never know when next you may have an opportunity to collect plants.

I recommend using white blotting paper as it shows up the shapes and colours of the flowers to better advantage than the green paper. It is a good idea to buy it in fairly large quantities from an office stationery shop, this being far less expensive than buying one or two sheets at a time. The blotting paper can be used several times, but must be replaced if it becomes discoloured or damp.

FLOWER PRESSES

To begin with you can press your flowers using the time-honoured method of placing the plants between sheets of blotting paper and then slipping them between the pages of a book. If you decide to start in this way then do choose a book that is heavy and fairly large, as using a small book will leave you with dozens of pieces of blotting paper containing only a few flowers. The blotting paper, when folded in half, should be slightly smaller than the pages of the book, and must be placed with the folded edge along the spine so that the blotting paper opens with the book. This method will give good results, but do make sure that you weigh the book down heavily, with the weight distributed evenly.

The flowers are created from dusky-pink ranunculus petals, with separated Queen Anne's lace florets in the centres. The leaves are those of a miniature rose. A plain brass frame would complement this picture perfectly.

Another good idea is to keep a few old telephone directories on hand. These can be used for flowers and leaves, but I find them really invaluable for pressing grasses, which would otherwise take up a great deal of space in my flower press. You need not use blotting paper in this instance because the paper used in telephone directories is absorbent and there is no danger of the print rubbing off on the grasses. Do be sure to leave several pages between the groups of plants.

The very best and most effective method of pressing plant material, however, is to use a flower press. Commercial flower presses are available from craft shops and, although they are good, I find that not only are they expensive, but they tend to be very small. I have a home-made flower press which gives excellent results and can be made easily and cheaply.

How to make your own press:
You will need four pieces of corrugated cardboard (the sides of a cardboard box are suitable); a few sheets of ordinary strong cardboard and sheets of blotting paper measuring 57 x 44,5 cm.

1. Cut the corrugated cardboard into four rectangles each measuring 25 x 32 cm.

2. Glue two rectangles together to form the top, and two together to form the base of the press.
3. Cut the ordinary cardboard into rectangles each measuring 22,5 x 30 cm.
4. Cut the sheets of blotting paper in half, and fold each half in two.
5. The top and bottom sections of corrugated cardboard can be covered with decorative floral wrap or press-on plastic film which gives the press an attractive finish.

How to use the press:
Place a piece of plain cardboard between each folder of blotting paper. This forms a protective layer and prevents any stems or thicker sections of one group of plants marking those in the next blotting paper folder.

If you run out of cardboard you can use several sheets of newspaper to act as a buffer between your plants. As a general rule, though, I wouldn't recommend it as it makes the press very bulky and untidy. Once the plants, blotting paper and cardboard are in position, tie two pieces of household elastic around the press, across and down, to secure it. This holds everything firmly in place and stretches to accommodate more layers of blotting paper and cardboard. It is also quick and easy to remove and re-

A set of pictures in which grey, blue and mauve flowers were used. The outlines are softened by dark blue lobelia sprays, lavender and santolina leaves and ferns. Most of the flowers are hydrangeas: the variety of shades created by pressing makes each picture different. Set on a white background with a pale grey mount, these pictures will look best with simple, white frames.

place when you want to put new specimens in your press (*see Fig. 1.1*).

I keep my flower press under a large pile of gramophone records, but heavy books or bricks will do just as well. Whatever type of press you use, make sure that the weight on the flower press is evenly distributed. If your flowers are very firmly pressed they dry faster and this helps them retain their shape and colour. Do remember to keep your press in a dry place, but not in the direct sunlight. Dampness is ruinous to both the press and the plant material.

PRESSING PLANTS ON HOLIDAY

Once you have been bitten by the flower collecting bug you will find yourself unable to resist the unusual and attractive plants you see when on holiday. Plan in advance by making a small, lightweight travelling press before you set out on your next trip.

Buy a small hardcover exercise book and cut your blotting paper so that, when folded in half, it is a little smaller all round than the book. Insert a folder of blotting paper between every fourth or fifth page. Start filling the book from the back and in order to prevent the plants from slipping out, tie a piece of

corrugated cardboard

ordinary cardboard
blotting paper folder containing plants
ordinary cardboard

Fig. 1.1

elastic firmly around the book. When it's not in use keep it under the heaviest object you can find. The telephone directories in your hotel room or even your suitcase will serve this purpose.

If you run out of blotting paper, two or three paper tissues make a good substitute in an emergency.

When you travel far afield in this country, or go overseas, it is worthwhile buying a small paperback guide to the local flora. This will enable you to identify the flowers and leaves that you collect. Once you have identified your flower, slip a note, with its name and where you found it, into the blotting paper folder. Plants that are unfamiliar to you can be difficult to identify at a later date – especially if their colour changes during pressing.

*A very natural and free-flowing picture in tones of cream, olive green and creamy pink.
To emphasise the design I did not add a border or mount and a plain, mid-brown frame with,
perhaps, a gold edge would create a completely harmonious picture. I used creamy-pink rose
petals for the flowers, with tiny alyssum florets in the centres. Dark green nandina leaves,
wild grasses and sprays of the very dainty variety of gypsophila complete the picture. It can be
very tempting in a picture of this kind to continue filling in spaces and spreading the design
out. Do take care to avoid this and keep your design simple and uncluttered.*

CHAPTER 2

Gathering Plants for Pressing

Once you start gathering material you will find that you acquire a deeper awareness of the beauty of nature and an ever increasing interest in the plants and flowers that are all around us and which we so often take for granted.

You will learn to notice the delicate markings and veinings of leaves, and see the exquisite, varying shades in a flower, where previously it was just a pretty colour. Even simple wild flowers and grasses take on new meaning and a Sunday afternoon walk can soon turn into a veritable treasure hunt.

As your interest in pressed flowers grows so will your desire to experiment with new plants. The extent of your collection will benefit from this interest and you will also be able to include unusual and interesting colours and shapes in your pictures.

FLOWERS

There are only two hard and fast rules that must be followed when collecting flowers. Firstly, be sure to pick specimens that are young and fresh – fully blown flowers are much more likely to fade. Secondly, never pick blooms that are damp, no matter how fresh they may look after a shower of rain. It can be tempting to press them before they are completely dry but this will only result in excessive fading and discoloration.

Single flat flowers (i.e. those that have only one layer of petals) such as phlox and primulas are perhaps the easiest flowers to begin with. These press very well and need the minimum of preparation. For flowers with several layers of petals such as roses, or those with large, thick centres, for example daisies, you will have to remove the petals and press them separately. Avoid collecting too many large flowers or petals as their very size makes them less useful – whereas, to go to the other extreme, you can never have enough tiny flowers.

Obviously it is not possible to grow all the types of flowers you might want to press in your own garden. I have never had success growing Queen Anne's lace, or the dainty white gypsophila, both of which are invaluable for pictures. So when these appear for sale on the flower stalls I buy a bunch of each, arrange some in a vase and press the rest! Another possibility is to collect flowers from a friend's garden. Send a thank-you card decorated with flowers from his or her garden – it will be greatly appreciated.

LEAVES

"Pressed Flowers" is really rather a misnomer, since you will obviously need far more than just flowers to create a picture. Leaves are equally important, as the correct leaves display the flowers to their best advantage and also add to the totally natural effect that you want to create. Sometimes it is possible to create a picture using only leaves. My pressed leaf file is as large as my flower file, since I find that you need leaves in as wide a variety of shapes, colours and sizes as possible.

Always try to collect several leaves equal in size and of similar colour of each variety. When you begin to make pictures you will find that you frequently need almost identical leaves to balance your design. This is, of course, particularly important if you are working on a geometric design. As well as single leaves, collect sprays of leaves,

Both of these are natural designs which I started with no preconceived plan. With the first design I kept to tones of cream and brown, using cosmos petals for the two large 'daisies'. With the cream mount a brown wooden frame would complete the colour theme. The other design could be called a 'garden' picture and I used phlox and hydrangeas with ferns, abelia, rue and feverfew leaves. A white frame would complement the white background and cream mount very well.

for example small rose or nandina leaves, and press them as a complete whole. As will be explained in Chapter 4, this can only be done if the stem is not too thick.

Grey leaves are always very useful; and the underside of some leaves, for example Cotoneaster, have a silvery-grey sheen which can be used to great advantage in pictures.

As with flowers, leaves can be collected throughout the year. Take advantage of the different foliage which appears as the seasons change. From the same tree you will often be able to pick soft, young green leaves in spring, darker green in summer, and, in many cases, beautifully coloured leaves in autumn.

As well as being able to choose from the infinite variety of colours to be found in leaves, there are also many different shapes to consider. Pointed, round, serrated – the list is almost endless, and your leaf file should contain as wide a variety as possible (*see Fig. 2.1*). Several plants have leaves that do not press as well as their flowers do, and it is important to look for substitute leaves that have a similar shape and colour. Leaves that do not press well at all are those which are thick and "fleshy" or, alternatively, leathery and dry to the touch.

Fig. 2.1

FERNS AND FRONDS

Ferns are a must for pressing, most types yielding good results. The soft, delicate varieties press more successfully, and are more useful than those which have an erect and rather stiff form of growth. Press whole fronds rather than individual leaves. You can always separate the leaves once they are pressed, but you may wish to use the frond as it is in a large picture. Very large sprays or fronds can be broken into smaller sections before pressing. Some trees, shrubs and flowers have dainty fern-like leaves, for example the California Poppy, so be on the lookout for these too.

A simple spray design using very few flowers. Hydrangea and phlox are used in the centre, while Queen Anne's lace, gypsophila and a spray of alyssum add height. Leaves of the maple tree form a background.

To create a softly natural effect in a picture, look for fronds of tiny flowers or buds, which usually appear on trees or shrubs in the spring.

GRASSES

Grasses are a valuable addition to your collection. They are extremely easy to press and can be found almost everywhere you look. It is not necessary to go out into the country to find them – they spring up along most pavements and, of course, in our gardens too! I sometimes go as far as to cultivate some grasses in my garden, waiting until they grow to the size I need!

Choose grasses that are delicate and fairly dainty. Those with thick and rather bulky heads press well but cause a problem when used in pictures as they prevent the glass from coming into contact with the flatter material.

STEMS, STAMENS AND TENDRILS

As most flowers and leaves are removed from their stalks before pressing, you will need a good collection of pressed stems to replace the originals. For this you must collect soft stems of varying thicknesses and lengths that will press flat. They often have gentle curves which give a very natural look to your design.

Finally, keep a small collection of tendrils and stamens as these play an important part in creating a natural look.

GATHERING

It is very important not to handle the plants more than you have to when you gather them. If you collect plants from your own garden and intend pressing them immediately, cut them over a shallow plastic or cardboard box, so that they can fall directly into it. Take care that you keep leaves and sprays apart from dainty or fragile flowers, thus preventing the latter from becoming bruised. If you have to wait before you begin pressing them, cut the plants with a longer stem and put them in a jar of water, which should be kept in a cool place.

When you go further afield to pick flowers, take along a plastic lunch box or ice-cream carton that you have lined with damp blotting paper. If the lid is firmly sealed the plants will remain fresh for some time.

Another good idea is to keep a plastic bag in your car in case you spot any pretty wild flowers alongside the road.

Place the plants in the bag and blow into it. Quickly tie a knot in the top, keeping in as much air as possible, and the plants will arrive home in good condition.

To suggest what time of day is best to collect material is not practical, as the opportunity to collect plants can arise at any time. I have found no significant difference in the final result of pressed plants which were collected at various times throughout the day. If you have no other choice than to pick plants early in the morning, when they may be damp with dew, then stand them in a jar of water for a few hours so that they have time to dry completely before you press them.

Always remember that it is important to plan ahead when you are collecting material. Many plants have short flowering seasons, and you must press enough to last right through the year. It's most frustrating to decide that a certain flower will add just the right touch to your picture, and then find that you have none left in your press and that you will have to wait until the next flowering season to gather more.

The following chapter gives a very rudimentary list of flowers and leaves suitable for pressing. They are, I think, generally well-known and often found in our gardens. You will soon find, however, that you want to experiment with new and different materials and that as you explore further afield you discover unexpected treasures.

An old-fashioned sampler, which makes a lovely gift for a special occasion, made entirely from flowers and leaves. It was great fun to make, and is something quite different from the usual flower designs.

CHAPTER 3

Flowers and Foliage for Pressing

The following list is by no means a comprehensive one of the plants that can be pressed but is intended as a guide to help you when you start out in this rewarding craft.

The choice of plant material for pressing is a very individual one, depending ultimately on the type of design that you find you prefer to do.

All the plants listed give good results when pressed and should provide you with a wide range of colours, textures and shapes. Only a very small percentage of plant material retains its original colour when pressed, and details of the various colour changes that occur in each plant have been included. To begin with don't collect great quantities of one plant; rather select several plants which will give you a good choice of colours, sizes and shapes.

As your interest grows you will definitely want to experiment with new plant material yourself. I am continually trying out new flowers and leaves for pressing from the wonderful choice of plants at our disposal.

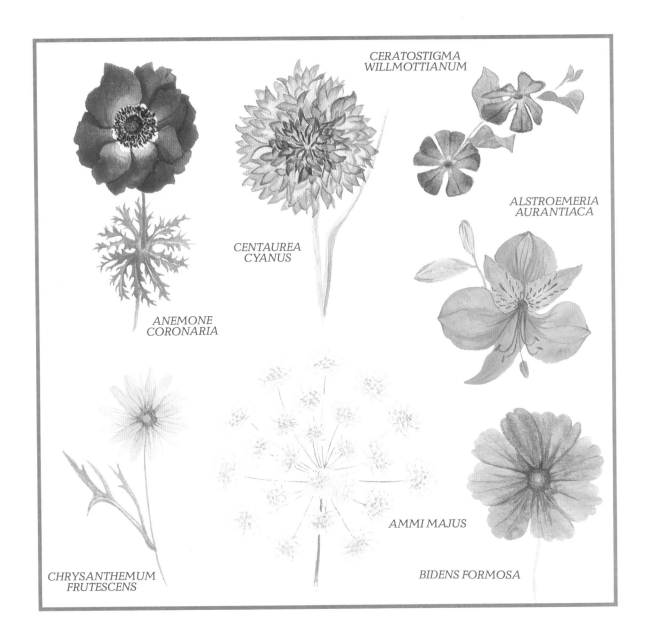

CERATOSTIGMA
WILLMOTTIANUM

ALSTROEMERIA
AURANTIACA

CENTAUREA
CYANUS

ANEMONE
CORONARIA

AMMI MAJUS

CHRYSANTHEMUM
FRUTESCENS

BIDENS FORMOSA

FLOWERS

AGAPANTHUS AFRICANUS
bulb: summer
Press flowers individually in profile, either in bud or fully open. Fades to a slightly paler blue.

ALSTROEMERIA AURANTIACA
(Peruvian Lily)
bulb: summer
Press petals separately – fades slightly to a creamy brown, and has beautiful markings and veins on the petals.

AMMI MAJUS **(Queen Anne's Lace)**
perennial: summer
Press some of the small heads separately and leave some attached to their stems. Invaluable when making pictures.

ANEMONE CORONARIA
bulb: later winter and spring
Clear bright colours which remain true. Separate the petals before pressing.

BAUHINIA GALPINII
shrub: summer
Petals of these brick-red flowers must be pressed separately. Very slight fading.

BIDENS
annual: autumn
Press its petals individually. Slight fading occurs, and white turns to pale cream.

BOUGAINVILLEA
climber: all year
Separate the petals. All colours (magenta, crimson, red and pink) are suitable for pressing. Almost no fading occurs.

CENTAUREA CYANUS
(Cornflower)
annual: summer
Divide into separate florets for pressing, and press in profile. Colour deepens slightly in both pink and blue.

CERATOSTIGMA WILLMOTTIANUM
(Chinese plumbago)
shrub: summer
Press the tiny blue flowers flat or in profile. Colour remains excellent.

CHRYSANTHEMUM FRUTESCENS
(Daisy bush)
shrub: spring/summer
Press the yellow, white or pink petals separately. Colour remains true.

CLIVIA MINIATA
bulb: spring
The orange/red petals of this beautiful flower must be pressed separately. Very slight fading occurs.

DAIS COTINIFOLIA
tree: spring
Pompom-like heads of flowers appear in spring. Press flowers separately in profile. The pale pink becomes a most attractive creamy-fawn.

IBERIS
UMBELLATA

GERANIUM

JASMINUM

GYPSOPHILA

EUPHORBIA
PULCHERRIMA

HEUCHERA
SANGUINEA

HYDRANGEA
MACROPHYLLA

DELPHINIUM
annual: summer
Press flowers individually. Their colour is excellent.

DIASCIA BARBERAE
perennial: summer
Press flowers flat or in profile. Fades to a slightly paler pink.

ERICA BOWIEANA (Heath)
shrub: summer
Press sprays in all colours but avoid very thick varieties.

ESCHSCHOLZIA CALIFORNICA (Californian Poppy)
annual: summer
Press the cream, yellow and orange petals separately. Colour does not fade.

EUPHORBIA PULCHERRIMA (Poinsettia)
shrub: summer
Petals must be pressed separately. They become a deep wine-red and can be used as leaves in pictures.

GERANIUM
perennial: all year
A wonderful variety of shades which retain their colour. Press the petals separately.

GYPSOPHILA
annual: summer
Different types vary in the size of their flowers – look out for all of them as they are very useful. Press in sprays.

HEUCHERA SANGUINEA (Coral Bells)
perennial: summer
Press the dainty sprays of pink and red flowers. Keeps colour well.

HYDRANGEA MACROPHYLLA
shrub: summer
Press each floret separately, face down. Blue flowers keep their colour well. Pink turns to a darker mauve-pink shade. Press some while they are still green. The excellent range of colours makes these flowers an invaluable addition to your collection.

IBERIS UMBELLATA (Candytuft)
annual: summer
Press whole heads of small florets in all shades – white, pink and lavender. White turns to pale cream.

IMPATIENS
perennial: all year
Presses well, but tends to loose some colour and become transparent.

JASMINUM (Jasmine)
climber: spring
Press the yellow or white flowers flat or in profile.

LANTANA MONTEVIDENSIS (Purple lantana)
shrub: all year
Low-growing variety with mauve flowers. Press the small flowers individually flat or in profile.

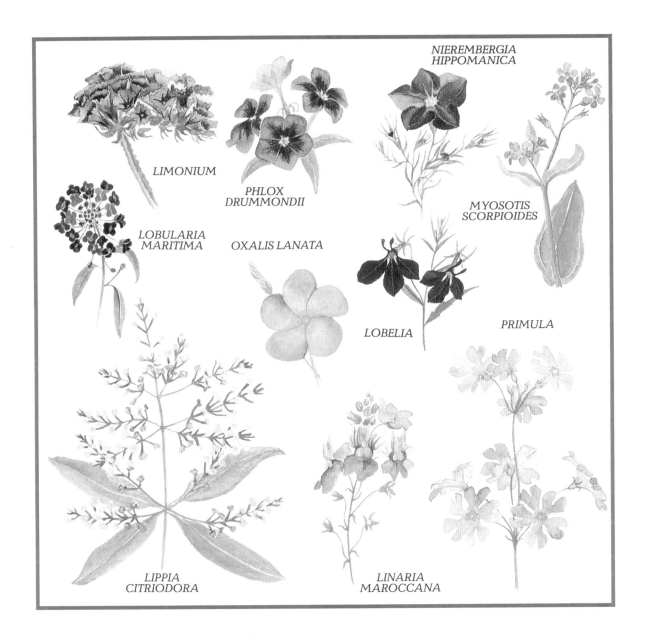

LIMONIUM

PHLOX
DRUMMONDII

NIEREMBERGIA
HIPPOMANICA

MYOSOTIS
SCORPIOIDES

LOBULARIA
MARITIMA

OXALIS LANATA

LOBELIA

PRIMULA

LIPPIA
CITRIODORA

LINARIA
MAROCCANA

LIMONIUM (Statice)
perennial: summer
Paper-like flowers in shades of white, blue and mauve. Press single florets in profile.

LINARIA MAROCCANA
annual: all year
Varied colours remain true. Press in profile.

LIPPIA CITRIODORA (Lemon Verbena)
shrub: summer
Press complete sprays of the tiny white flowers which appear in early summer.

LOBELIA
annual: summer
Press single flowers and small sprays. Remains a true blue.

LOBULARIA MARITIMA
(Alyssum)
annual: all year
Press whole heads with the stem. Keeps its colours (white, pink, blue and mauve) well. The tiny florets can be used to recreate the centre of a flower.

MYOSOTIS SCORPIOIDES
(Forget-me-not)
perennial: summer
All shades of blue remain true. Press single flowers and small sprays.

NIEREMBERGIA HIPPOMANICA
perennial: summer
Press flowers and small sprays of buds. The flowers can be pressed flat or in profile.

ORNITHOGALUM THYRSOIDES
(Chincherinchee)
bulb: spring
Separate the flowers and press them flat and in profile. The creamy white flowers tend to fade slightly.

OXALIS LANATA
perennial: spring
Dainty pink or white flowers with clover-like leaves. Press buds and flowers separately, or in sprays.

PENTAS
shrub: summer
Varying shades of pink and red florets. Press each floret separately, face down. Colour tends to deepen.

PETREA VOLUBILIS
climber: spring, autumn
Press face down. Their deep purple-blue colour does not fade.

PHLOX DRUMMONDII
annual: all year
Wide range of colours which all remain true. Press flowers face down and in profile, and also press some buds. Very useful for pictures.

PLUMBAGO AURICULATA
climber: summer
Pale blue flowers which fade slightly. Press individually, flat or in profile.

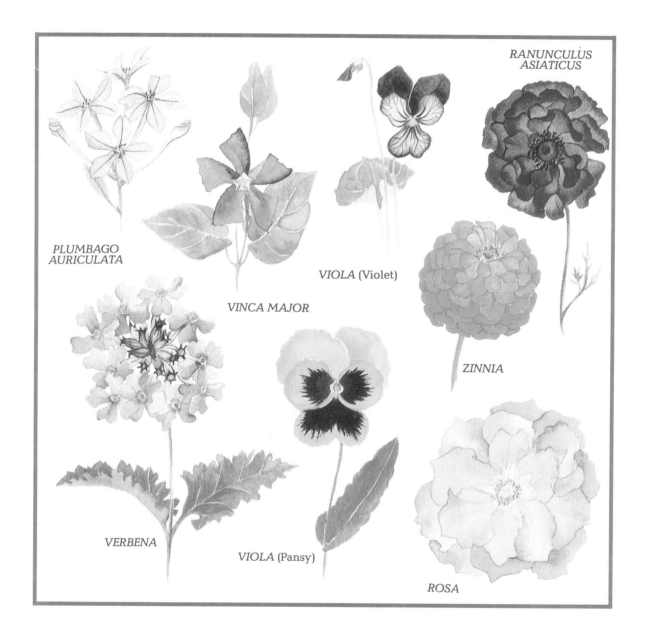

PLUMBAGO
AURICULATA

VINCA MAJOR

VIOLA (Violet)

RANUNCULUS
ASIATICUS

ZINNIA

VERBENA

VIOLA (Pansy)

ROSA

PRIMULA
annual: winter/spring
Press both purple and white, face-down and in profile. White becomes pale cream. Press some buds while they are still attached to the calyx and stem.

PRUNUS
(Brown-leafed plum)
tree: spring
Press the dainty pink blossoms face down and in profile.

RANUNCULUS ASIATICUS
bulb: winter/spring
Remove petals and press them separately. Colours remain true. The reverse side of the petals can be used with great effect.

ROSA
climbers, hybrid teas, floribundas: spring/summer
Press petals of almost all the smaller varieties. White petals turn cream and other colours fade very slightly.

TECOMARIA CAPENSIS
(Cape Honeysuckle)
climber: summer
Press sprays of buds and single flowers in profile.

VERBENA
perennial groundcover and annual variety: summer
Press florets separately. Various pinks, mauve and white all keep their colour.

VINCA MAJOR (Periwinkle)
shrub or groundcover: summer
Press flat or in profile – an excellent blue.

VIOLA (Pansies and violets)
annual: winter
Small flowers can be pressed whole; separate the petals of larger flowers. Remove as much of the stalk as possible and press the flowers face down.

ZINNIA
annual: summer
Wide variety of shades in the pink, orange and red range. Press petals separately. Reverse side of the petals is also most attractive.

LEAVES

ABELIA GRANDIFLORA (Glossy Abelia)
shrub
Evergreen shrub with small leaves ranging from green to reddish-brown. Press young leaves taken from the ends of branches.

ACER (Maple)
tree
Press throughout the year as the colours change. Very useful shape and colour stays true.

ANTHEMIS CUPANIANA (Chamomile)
herb
Feathery leaves which press well and can be used to replace leaves of other daisy varieties.

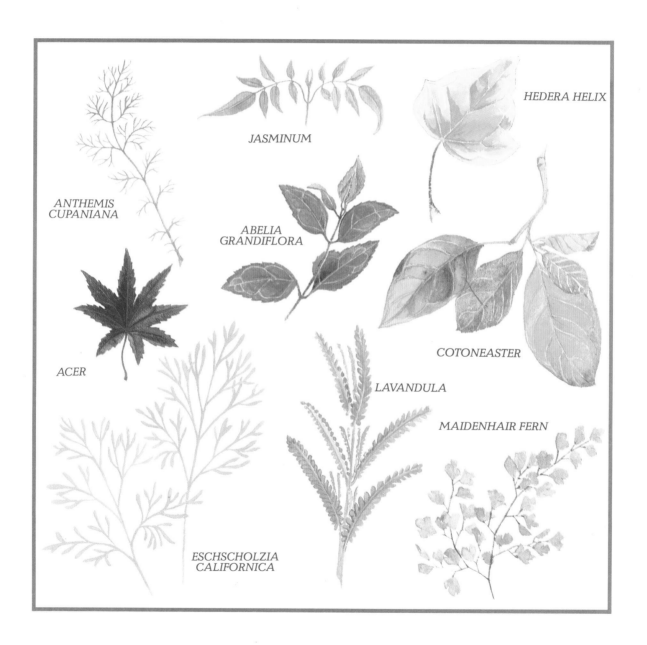

JASMINUM

HEDERA HELIX

ANTHEMIS
CUPANIANA

ABELIA
GRANDIFLORA

ACER

COTONEASTER

LAVANDULA

MAIDENHAIR FERN

ESCHSCHOLZIA
CALIFORNICA

CENTAUREA
perennial
Attractive grey-white leaves which keep their colour when pressed.

CERATOSTIGMA WILLMOTTIANUM
shrub
Press small leaves in the autumn when lovely shades of red appear.

CHRYSANTHEMUM PARTHENIUM (Feverfew)
herb: all year
Attractively shaped leaves which press well.

COTONEASTER
shrub
Press the tiny leaves in early summer. The reverse side has an attractive silvery-grey sheen which is most useful.

ESCHSCHOLZIA CALIFORNICA (Californian Poppy)
annual
Soft grey fern-like leaves – press in quantity.

EUONYMUS
shrub
Evergreen with small plain or variegated leaves that press very well.

FERNS
perennial
Except for the large sword fern, almost all varieties press well and the colours stay true. Very useful.

HEDERA HELIX (English Ivy)
climber
Press young, small leaves of variegated and green ivy. Larger leaves tend to turn brown.

HYDRANGEA MACROPHYLLA
shrub
Press small young leaves. They have most attractive veining and remain a soft green.

HYPERICUM
shrub
Low-growing shrub with variegated green and cream leaves that are sometimes tinged with red.

JASMINUM (Jasmine)
climber
Press the small green leaves individually.

LANTANA MONTEVIDENSIS (Purple lantana)
shrub: all year
The leaves of this shrub are fine and fern-like and press very well.

LAVANDULA (Lavender)
shrub
Long grey leaves with excellent colour. Press in quantity.

NANDINA DOMESTICA (Heavenly or Sacred Bamboo)
shrub
Green leaves in summer and varying shades of pinks and reds in autumn. Press complete sprays as well as individual leaves.

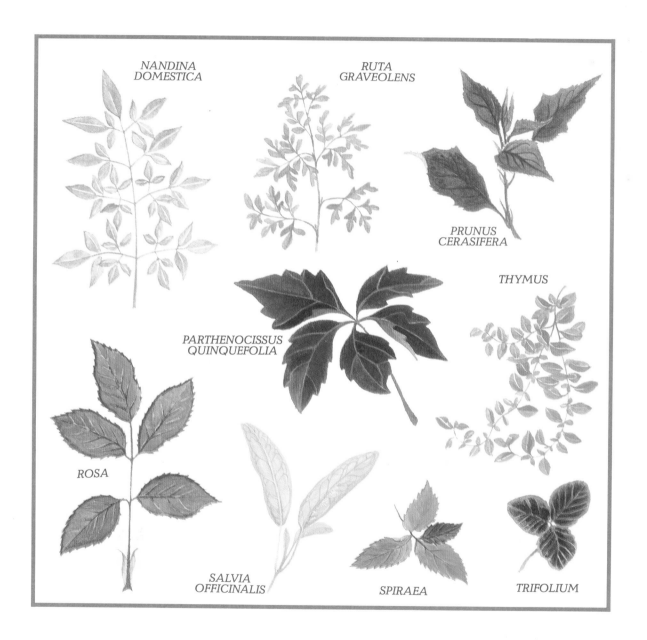

NANDINA
DOMESTICA

RUTA
GRAVEOLENS

PRUNUS
CERASIFERA

THYMUS

PARTHENOCISSUS
QUINQUEFOLIA

ROSA

SALVIA
OFFICINALIS

SPIRAEA

TRIFOLIUM

PARSLEY
herb
The dark curly leaves and stems press well
and keep their colour.

**PARTHENOCISSUS QUINQUEFOLIA
(Virginia Creeper)**
climber
Beautiful autumn colours. Press small
leaves and sprays.

PRUNUS CERASIFERA (Flowering Plum)
tree
Dark purple-brown leaves. Try to pick in
spring when the leaves are soft.

ROSA
shrub/climber
Press leaves of every type of rose in
quantity as they all vary slightly. Some
varieties even have a slight reddish tinge.
Press complete stalks of smaller leaves.

RUTA GRAVEOLENS (Rue)
herb
Scented herb with blue-grey divided leaves.
Colour is retained.

SALVIA OFFICINALIS (Sage)
herb
Herb with pointed grey-green leaves, which
press well and are most useful.

SANTOLINA CHAMAECYPARISSUS
shrub
Feathery grey-white leaves which retain
their colour very well.

SPIRAEA (Red May)
shrub
Wide variety of shadings in these leaves
which press well.

THYMUS (Thyme)
herb
Press whole sprays of these tiny green,
variegated leaves.

TRIFOLIUM (Clover)
perennial
Leaves of both the green and purple/black
varieties press very well.

GRASSES

We have such a variety of wild grasses
that to list them would be an almost im-
possible task. Try to pick grass when it is
young when the seeds are less likely to
fall. Avoid those with very thick stems.
Also press long thin blades of grass from
your lawn before it is mown.

STEMS

You will need a good collection of stems
to replace those you have removed from
your flowers. Press stems of soft, thin
grasses, violets, clover, small daisies and
sweet pea tendrils.

CHAPTER 4

Preparing, Pressing and Storing

To preserve the beauty of the plants after you have collected them, it is well worth your while to take extra care when you prepare and press them.
No great skill is needed but a little patience and attention to detail will be amply rewarded by the final results. When you set out to gather plants make sure that you will have enough time shortly thereafter to prepare and press them. Careful storage of your plants after they have been pressed is equally important, so follow the guidelines given in this chapter carefully. The ultimate success of your pictures will very much depend on the care that you take at this stage.

PREPARING

Most of the plant material you gather will need a certain amount of preparation before it is ready for pressing. This is not as difficult or as time-consuming as you may imagine, and the final results will more than repay the care and effort involved.

Flowers with an open form and a single layer of petals, for example primulas, are very easy to press. Using a pair of small, sharp scissors snip off the stalk as close to the base of the flower as possible (*see Fig. 4.1*), and, as you will press most of the flowers face down or "open", remove any part of the calyx that still remains (when the stem is cut not all of the calyx comes away with the stem — small sections cling to the petals and must be carefully removed). A small proportion of the flowers, especially the tiny ones, should be pressed in profile or "sideways", thus giving them the appearance of a bud. In this case cut the stem off slightly further down and do not remove the calyx (*see Fig. 4.2*). You will find that there are some flowers, such as cornflowers and linaria, which really only press well in profile, and with these you don't need to remove the stem — providing, of course, that it is not too thick. When pressing flowers in pro-file, the stem extends below the petals and will not cause an indentation on them. When preparing flowers such as hydrangeas or verbenas, which consist of a large head of florets, each floret must be cut off and pressed separately.

In the case of flowers with several layers of petals, roses and ranunculus for example, the petals must be removed and separated for pressing (*see Fig. 4.3*). This also applies to flowers with very thick centres such as daisies. When the petals are dry they can be re-assembled into the original flower shape.

With leaves it is best to remove any stalks before pressing. The only exceptions are sprays of dainty leaves on a thin stem. In the case of larger sprays, remove the leaves from the stem and place them on the blotting paper in their original arrangement. Another stem can be used when you re-construct the dried spray.

When pressing grasses, ferns or flower sprays with long stems, place them on the blotting paper in their natural shapes (*see Fig. 4.4*). Don't try to straighten them, as the natural curves will give a far more realistic look to your finished picture. The same rule applies to soft stems; if these are left out of water for about half an hour they will curve even more.

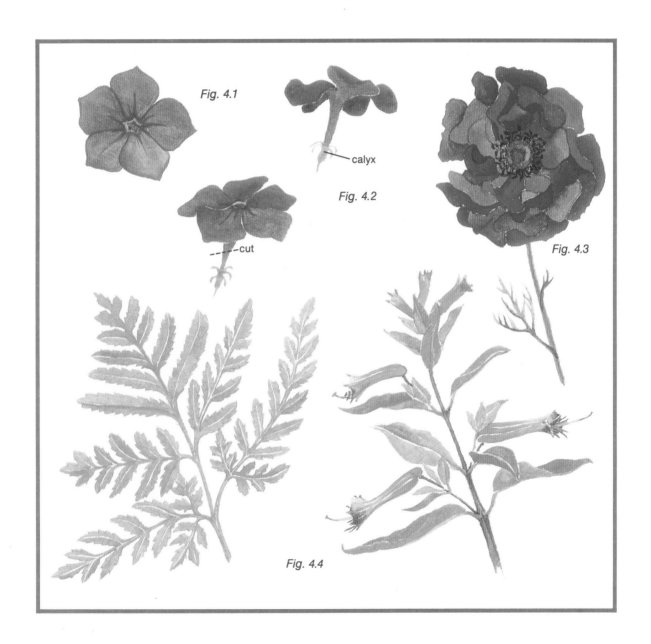

Fig. 4.1

calyx

Fig. 4.2

cut

Fig. 4.3

Fig. 4.4

A final tip, which applies to all the material you press, is to check that there are no tiny insects such as aphids lurking about. They can cause most unwelcome and unsightly marks and blotches on your pressed plants.

PRESSING

The preparation and pressing of plants really go hand in hand, as it is important to get everything into the press as quickly as possible. Lay a sheet of blotting paper on the base-board of your press before you even start preparing your material and as you prepare the plants place them directly onto the blotting paper thereby ensuring the minimum of handling.

Make sure that the plants do not touch each other – but, at the same time, don't be afraid to use all the available space. For example, you should be able to get 30 to 40 hydrangea florets on one blotting paper folder. Sometimes you will have to press a flower down with the ball of your finger to encourage it to have a certain shape, particularly when pressing in profile.

To ensure that plants receive the same pressure and therefore dry at the same rate, keep flowers of a similar thickness in the same folder of blotting paper.

This, of course, applies to other plant material as well. Close the folder over the plants, and then cover it with a piece of plain cardboard.

Continue to press your plant material in this way, remembering to slip a piece of paper, on which you have written the date and type of flower being pressed, into each layer. A little organisation

Greenish-white hydrangeas, phlox, primulas, gypsophila and Queen Anne's lace have been used with a variety of fern-like leaves.

In the plate on the left: gypsophila, ferns and Queen Anne's lace soften this design of mauve and pink shades. The natural design on the right has oriental undertones which were achieved by using the reverse side of ranunculus petals; and also geranium petals, grasses, nandina and red may leaves.

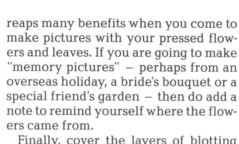

reaps many benefits when you come to make pictures with your pressed flowers and leaves. If you are going to make "memory pictures" – perhaps from an overseas holiday, a bride's bouquet or a special friend's garden – then do add a note to remind yourself where the flowers came from.

Finally, cover the layers of blotting paper and cardboard with the top board, secure with elastic and place the flower press under weights.

A good place in which to keep your press is in a cupboard in a sunny room.

Never leave it in direct sunlight or any very warm place as the petals will then dry out too quickly and become very brittle.

We now come to one of the most important factors in the successful pressing of plants – and that is patience. The plants *must* be left for five to six weeks before they can be used, so do resist the temptation to peek at your plants every few days! If you keep the press in a warm place that is free of damp, the plants will dry more rapidly and keep their colour better.

A summer garden – with various flowers and grasses 'growing' from a base of several types of leaves.

STORING

Once your flowers, leaves and stems are dry you will want to remove them from the flower press to make space for new material.

Cut a sheet of blotting paper down the centre and fold each section in half. Great care must be taken in transferring the plants, as they will have become very delicate and sometimes brittle. I use the extended blade of a sharp hobby knife, sliding it very gently under the flower, easing it off the blotting paper and transferring it on the blade to the fresh paper. When you have moved all the flowers, fold the top section of the blotting paper over the dry specimens. This forms a simple file in which to store pressed material.

Write details of the flowers on a small tab and attach it to the right-hand corner. Attach each following tab a little to the left of the last one, and you will be able to see at a glance which "file" you need. I keep all my dried material in two large box files which can be purchased from any stationer.

As your collection grows you will have to evolve a definite method of filing your plants. Flowers which I press in large quantities, such as hydrangeas or phlox, have a file, sometimes several, to themselves. Smaller quantities of dried material are filed together with labels such as "small blue flowers" or "red and pink petals". For leaves I follow the same procedure. Rose leaves and ferns, for example, are kept in their own separate files, whilst others go under headings such as "small green leaves" or "large autumn colours". I have found this system works very well, as I can lay my hands on what I need almost immediately, without having to hunt through all the other files.

Remember that the drying process continues even after the plants appear to be dry, and the longer they are left undisturbed, the less likely they are to fade.

You may find that some plants become badly creased or discoloured during pressing, and it's best to be ruthless and discard these, as they will just take up valuable storage space. If, however, only one petal is damaged, keep the flower. The other petals can be used to replace any which are broken during handling, or the whole flower may be used in a picture where a leaf curves over the damaged section. In certain instances a petal or leaf that has been slightly creased or bent back can be used to advantage to create a completely natural effect.

CHAPTER 5

Backgrounds and Frames

The background and frame of your picture must be chosen with great care. They both form such an integral part of the design that it can be said that the final result is as dependent on these two factors as it is on the flowers themselves.

In some instances the design and colour of your picture will be the factors that influence your choice of background and frame, and at other times you may have an unusual frame or a particularly attractive background and these will determine your picture design. The correct background is, of course, as important for items such as cards and lampshades.

Always remember that there should be a completely harmonious balance between the design, background and frame.

BACKGROUNDS

Paper and mounting card are the most frequently used backgrounds, with fabric being an alternative when you want to create a special effect. Paper is probably most commonly used and when you start shopping around you will find that there is a very wide choice of both colours and textures. Always remember that it is most important to use the best quality paper, the expense being far outweighed by its appearance and lasting quality. And don't forget that you will probably be able to use one sheet of paper for several pictures.

For white or off-white backgrounds there is a wide variety of drawing and watercolour paper available. For coloured backgrounds I find the best paper is Canson Mi-Teintes pastel paper, which comes in a wide range of shades and does not fade. Smooth or finely-textured papers are best, as a too-rough texture can cause marks on delicate flowers and leaves.

When you choose paper for the background do check the texture on both sides as it is often different. I have found that even the colour of some paper varies very slightly on the different sides owing to the change in texture. This is a point to watch, particularly when you are making two or three pictures in a matching set.

Mounting board is available in many attractive shades and its completely smooth surface can be very effective in some designs.

An unusual but extremely attractive background is parchment. The great interest now shown in calligraphy means that parchment is easily obtainable and there are several pastel shades available as well as the more conventional "natural" colours. It can be purchased in quite small sheets which are very useful for making just one special picture. Paper, mounting card and parchment can all be obtained at art shops and selected stationers.

Fabric can be used as a background for flower pictures, but it requires more preparation than paper. It is easy to cut paper to fit the frame, but more care must be taken with fabric as its weave must be absolutely straight. In other words, the threads must be completely horizontal and vertical. You will need to back it with a piece of iron-on stiffener in order to give it body, or, alternatively, you can glue the cloth onto a piece of cardboard. Use a clear glue – I would suggest Bostik Clear Adhesive – and place glue only on the outer edge of the cardboard. Take care to smooth it down

Three very different designs which show how, in each example, plants, backgrounds and frames have been used to create a harmonious picture.

well and again make sure that the weave of the fabric is straight. The best fabrics to use are finely-woven linens and light-weight furnishing fabrics – but take care that the texture is not so rough that it will mark the flowers.

FRAMES

When you choose a frame you must remember that it has to harmonise with your picture and never draw the eye away from the design. The colour, style and shape of the frame must all complement the picture. To find the right frame is not really difficult, as many department stores and craft shops stock ready-made frames in a wide variety of colours, sizes and styles.

Before you even start your picture I would suggest that you make enquiries about, and note down, the sizes of various frames. This will enable you to plan your design on the correct size background – you must never cut your card or paper until you are absolutely certain of your frame size.

The colour of the frame is also going to play a very important role and, again, this does not necessarily present a problem. Frames are available in several woodgrain finishes plus a few colours, mainly cream, white and beige. How-

ever the plain, unvarnished wooden frames can easily be painted in any colour you choose. Spray paint is probably the easiest to use, but it can be rather expensive if you need several colours.

I find that poster paint works very well and with a few jars of the basic colours you can mix any shade you want (Pelikan Plaka is an excellent poster paint and is available from stationers and art shops). First rub the frame down with sandpaper to remove any rough patches and then apply three coats of paint, allowing time for each coat to dry thoroughly. Finally, apply a coat of polyurethane matt varnish to protect the paint.

Modern clip frames, which have no surround, are also extremely effective when used for certain designs, although obviously are not suited to a design such as a Victorian posy.

Silver and brass photograph frames can be used to make enchanting flower pictures. They tend to be rather expensive, so be on the lookout for them at sales and secondhand shops.

Generally speaking, avoid very ornate and gilded frames. No matter how striking they are, there is a danger that the attraction of the frame will compete with the beauty of your flowers rather than complementing them.

Many ready-made frames have a hardboard or masonite backing, but there are some that only come with a thin piece of cardboard behind the glass. In this case a piece of strong corrugated cardboard, cut to fit the frame, will serve to back the picture very well. The actual process of framing of your picture will be dealt with in the next chapter.

An old-fashioned circlet design using a wide variety of flowers and leaves.

CHAPTER 6

Creating a Picture

*O*ne of the delights of making pressed flower pictures is that you are able to create attractive designs without being especially artistic. Probably the easiest way to start out on a new project is to study existing designs and use them as a basis for your first pictures. The flowers you use, the colours and the tiny details you add will, however, make the picture uniquely yours.
For natural pictures your own garden will provide inspiration, but you will also get many ideas from such sources as floral greeting cards, giftwrap, embroidery designs and even fabrics.
Start a scrapbook of floral designs and you will have an immediate source of ideas and inspiration for your pictures.

COLOUR

The choice and blending of colours is a very individual matter and, as well as your own personal preference, a great many factors will influence the colours you use in your pictures.

You may want to make a picture for a room that is entirely furnished in blues and greens, or, perhaps, a card for a golden wedding anniversary using mainly cream and yellow flowers.

In the beginning the plants that are readily available for you to press will limit your colour choice. Later, as you go further afield, and expand your collection, the whole spectrum of colours will be at your fingertips and you will have to be more selective.

Rather than choose plants by their actual colour I suggest that you look at the depth of colour. By this I mean that you will need flowers from the palest to the deepest shades of a colour — but avoid the very intense, sharp colours such as shocking pink. Cream, white and pastel shades will all blend together with very pleasing results and the slightly darker shades of the foliage you use will give the necessary emphasis to your design and bring out the colours of the flowers.

Vivid colours such as orange, bright yellow and red are difficult to use suc-

An oval posy design in shades of blue using hydrangeas, cornflowers, verbena, primula and ceratostigma. Ferns and gypsophila add softening touches.

cessfully. Whilst not ruling them out altogether, I suggest that you use them with caution and when you do, keep your design very simple and fairly small. You can also soften the effect when using rather bright colours by introducing white or cream flowers into the design.

Dark shades, as opposed to bright ones, form an essential part of your collection. You are attempting to create the same harmonious blend of colours that you find in nature and therefore need the various depths of colour. Remember that, visually, dark colours retreat and pale colours come forward, so try and balance the contrasting colours evenly in your picture. If all your pastel shades are on one side and dark colours on the opposite side, your picture will be distressing to the eye, and the design itself will fade into total insignificance.

The background colour that you choose is going to be an integral part of your design and must be chosen with great care. As with the flowers, avoid using very bright or startling colours.

A dark brown or green background is ideal for displaying the colour and form of cream, white or grey plants to their best advantage and, in the same way, dark colours can be very effectively laid on a pale background. Do be careful,

though, not to use very vivid material on a contrasting background. This tends to create an "op-art" effect, which is the very antithesis of the natural material you are using.

A geometric design using autumn-hued nandina leaves and poinsettia petals, with red rose and alstroemeria petals in the centre.

A blend of flowers and background can be very pleasing – for example, pale blue flowers and silvery leaves on a darker blue backing, or varying shades of pink on soft pink parchment. Select a few different shades of background papers and by placing the flowers on them you will find which one creates the most attractive effect.

As is the case with fabrics, wallpaper and paint, a certain amount of fading will occur over a period of time. Allowance must be made for this – so don't use cream flowers on a white background, or they may eventually disappear altogether! To prevent excessive fading hang your pictures with their backs to the light and never on a sunny wall. If you are planning to give your picture to a friend do include a note to this effect.

PICTURE DESIGN

Whether you are working from another picture or starting from scratch, begin with a simple design, using only a few flowers and leaves. Start off by measuring and lightly marking the centrepoint on the paper and, as you lay your plants in place, keep checking that your margins are equal and your design is well balanced (*see Fig. 6.1*).

Don't be in a hurry to glue the plants in place, but allow yourself time to try various arrangements, gently moving the plants around until you are happy with the result. Avoid harsh, straight lines; remember that gentle curves will give the most natural effect to your picture. Don't overcrowd your picture or feel that you have to fill the whole frame. At the same time, bear in mind that a small arrangement of flowers in a large frame is as unattractive. The importance of balance between design, background and frame cannot be over-emphasised.

A formal design, e.g. a posy, is perhaps one of the easiest to do. A basic shape and outline already exists and your skill can be concentrated on filling in the design. Begin by laying down a few leaves

Fig. 6.1 centre line

keep opposite margins equal

I have tried to use the varying blue, mauve and grey-blue shades of hydrangea flowers to create a misty and subtle feeling in this picture. The silvery-grey leaves of sage, santolina and centaurea blend with the flowers and mount.

to form the outline and then position the central flower or focal point. Now you can start to fill in, from the centre outwards, with flowers and leaves. Finally add small sprays and buds to soften the outline and balance the design (*see Fig. 6.2*).

A more natural design is very much a matter of individual taste and it is, therefore, not really possible to say exactly how and where you should begin. Often the plants you have will, by their very shape and form, help to formulate a design. I have often found that pictures with no preconceived plan turn out to be the most rewarding. It is sometimes helpful to leave a picture for a while and return to it later with fresh eyes – possibly then discovering where a few changes are necessary.

Geometric designs are fun to do and give you more scope to use contrasting colours. Leaves, which have such an incredible variety of shapes, can be used most successfully in this type of picture. These designs have the advantage of looking very attractive hanging in a man's study or office, where a more obviously "flowery" picture would be less appropriate. Once again, the plants themselves will inspire you. You will need several duplicate leaves or flowers, and extra care must be taken in measuring when making your picture (*see Fig. 6.3*).

After a while you may find yourself becoming stale – absolutely stumped for new ideas and just repeating designs, with only a few changes here and there. Take a break, and, after a week or two, you will come back to your picture filled with new inspiration.

Fig. 6.2

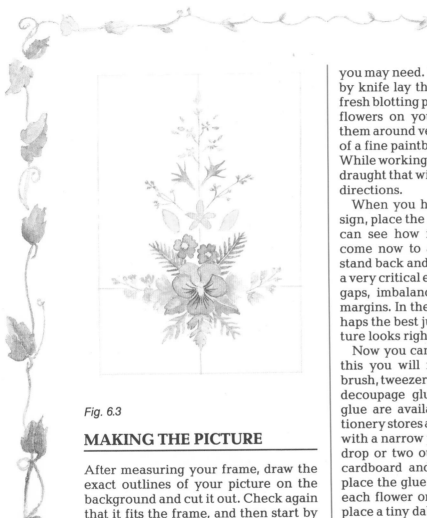

Fig. 6.3

MAKING THE PICTURE

After measuring your frame, draw the exact outlines of your picture on the background and cut it out. Check again that it fits the frame, and then start by taking out a selection of the flowers, leaves, sprays and stems that you think you may need. Using the blade of a hobby knife lay them gently on a piece of fresh blotting paper. Start arranging the flowers on your background, moving them around very carefully with the tip of a fine paintbrush, or your fingernail. While working be careful of any sudden draught that will blow your design in all directions.

When you have completed your design, place the frame over it so that you can see how it will finally look. We come now to a very important point: stand back and study your picture with a very critical eye. Look for any obvious gaps, imbalance of colour or uneven margins. In the final test the eye is perhaps the best judge as to whether a picture looks right and is well balanced.

Now you can start glueing – and for this you will need a very fine paintbrush, tweezers and either white glue or decoupage glue. Both these types of glue are available from craft and stationery stores and come in a small bottle with a narrow pointed spout. Squeeze a drop or two out onto a spare piece of cardboard and use the paintbrush to place the glue on the plant. Gently lift each flower or leaf with the tweezers, place a tiny dab of glue on the back and lightly press it into place on the background. Place the glue in the centre of

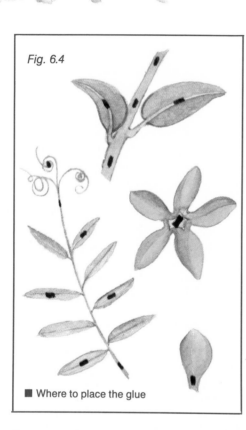

Fig. 6.4

■ Where to place the glue

with a piece of blotting paper and then the glass from the frame. If left unprotected the flowers will absorb moisture and start to curl.

FRAMING

Once your picture is completed place it straight into the frame. The flowers must come into contact with the glass, so that condensation does not form. If your picture is to be placed in a mount, care must be taken not to use thick mounting board, as this will prevent the glass from lying directly on the flowers.

Your picture must be free of any dust or tiny seeds, so either brush away any specks with a paint brush or blow, very gently, to remove them. Place the clean glass over the picture, holding it at the edges to prevent any fingermarks. Place the frame over the glass and picture. Cut a piece of plain smooth card to the same size as the backing. Whether the latter is hardboard or corrugated cardboard you will need this card to protect the picture.

Carefully turn the picture over, fit the card and then the backing into place. To hold this in position you will need very small panel pins or staples and must push them into the frame with the flat blade of a pair of scissors (*see Fig. 6.5*). To

flowers, and at the base of individual petals. On the back of leaves and stems place tiny dabs of glue along the centre line (*see Fig. 6.4*).

If you have to leave your picture at any time before it is completed, cover it

prevent any dust from getting into the picture, place strips of masking tape which cover the gap between the backing and the frame around the edges. For a really professional-looking finish you can completely cover the back with brown paper.

Fig. 6.5

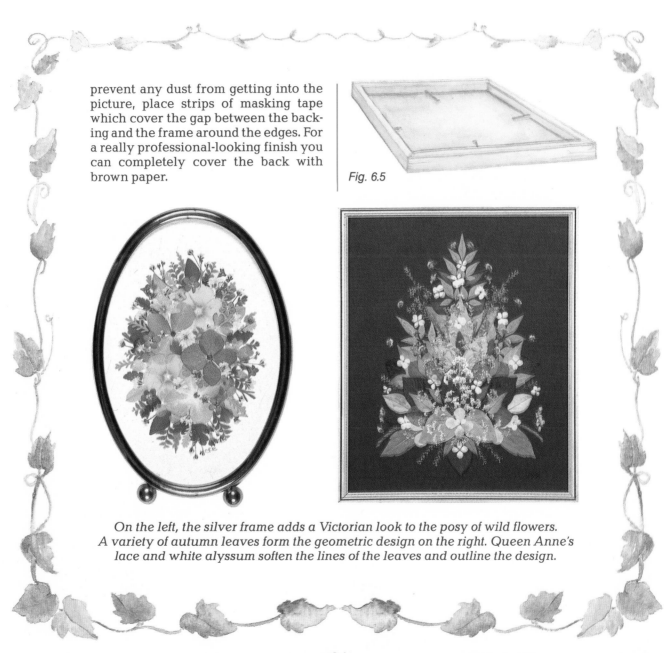

On the left, the silver frame adds a Victorian look to the posy of wild flowers. A variety of autumn leaves form the geometric design on the right. Queen Anne's lace and white alyssum soften the lines of the leaves and outline the design.

CHAPTER 7

Flower Crafts

When you have a good selection of pressed flowers you will have at your fingertips the materials to make a wide range of truly charming and decorative items.

Beautiful greeting cards, gift tags and bookmarks are quick and easy to make, and are sure to be kept and treasured by the recipient. Cards for special occasions will give enormous pleasure. Tiny decorated place cards at a special dinner will provide each guest with a memento. You can also use your flowers to decorate the covers of photograph albums, address books and diaries.

Flower-decorated trinket boxes make a delightful gift, being both pretty and practical. Small, attractive boxes are available at many gift shops, or alternatively you could cover a tiny plain box with gift wrap.

Lampshades decorated with pressed flowers are quite beautiful and this is, perhaps, one of the most attractive ways of displaying the delicate charm of pressed flowers. The glow of the light enhances the various shades and shapes of the plants.

CARDS, CALENDARS AND PLACE CARDS

Cards

When you make cards choose a good quality paper – again I would recommend Canson pastel paper. You will also need a ruler, a set square, a hobby knife, a pair of scissors and matt plastic film. The latter is available from hardware stores and craft shops. Bear in mind the size of the envelopes you have, or can obtain, before deciding on the size of your card. For an envelope 11,5 x 16 cm the size of the paper when folded should be 11 x 15 cm. For this card draw out a rectangle measuring 15 x 22 cm.

1. Cut out the card and lightly mark the centre or fold line.
2. Score lightly down this line with a hobby knife and fold the card in half.
3. Choose a different colour paper for the section on which you will arrange the flowers. Measure and cut this second piece making it slightly smaller all round (for example, 13 x 9 cm). If desired, draw a border around it with a felt-tip pen.
4. Following the instructions given in the previous chapter, arrange your flowers and glue them down.
5. Cover the card on which the flowers are arranged with a piece of matt plastic film, and ensure that you press it down very well.
6. Trim the edges of the film and glue the flower card to the base card, making sure it is in the centre and that the margins are equal.

Calendars

More or less the same procedure is followed to make a calendar, but, obviously, using only a single sheet of paper. Glue the finished picture onto a piece of strong cardboard cut to the same size as the picture and glue the date pad below the picture.

Place cards

Place cards are great fun to make, are always much admired and add a special touch to your table.

1. For each one, cut your paper – I would once again suggest Canson pastel paper or very lightweight card – to measure 8 x 9 cm and fold the card or paper in half.
2. Make a tiny arrangement of flowers and leaves on one section of the card and write in the guest's name.
3. Cover the entire front section of the place card with plastic film and trim the edges.

Trinket & Jewellery Boxes

Small, medium or large, there is no end to the usefulness of boxes. And now, with your new skill, you can turn them into charming containers, which can be displayed with pride.

If you have plain, prettily coloured boxes, then all you need to do is decorate the top with flowers. If, however, the box is rather dull, cover it first with an attractive floral gift wrap.

1. To decorate your box, choose a piece of matching background paper and cut it slightly smaller all round than the size of the top of the box.
2. Choose flowers that either blend in with, or repeat the colours on the box and arrange your design on the paper.
3. When you have completed it, cover the design with matt plastic film and carefully trim away excess around the edges.
4. Glue the paper to the top of the box.

To make a special jewellery box, such as the one shown in the photograph, you will need a sheet of strong cardboard measuring 64 x 51 cm; a set square; giftwrap of your choice; plain background paper; clear Bostik; a pair of scissors; a pair of compasses; a hobby knife; and clear matt plastic film.

To make the six-sided or hexagonal base, draw a circle with a radius of 11 cm. Mark the radius six times around the circle from any point on the circumference. With a ruler, connect the six points to form the hexagon. Using the set square, draw lines at right angles to the sides of the hexagon. Mark the lines off at 5 cm, and join them together. Add a flap measuring 1 cm to each outer section.

For the lid follow the same instructions but make the radius 11,5 cm and omit the sides.

1. Following the diagram (see Fig. 7.1) cut the cardboard along the solid lines and score along the dotted lines.
2. To make the base fold up the sides marked "A" on the diagram and glue the flaps marked "B" on the diagram to each adjacent side.
3. Attach the cut-out lid to the base with an extra strip of paper measuring 10 x 9 cm as shown in the diagram.
4. Cover the box with giftwrap and decorate the top with pressed flowers using the same method described for the small boxes.
5. Glue giftwrap to the inside of the lid – and, for added strength, glue a second piece of cardboard neatly trimmed under the base.

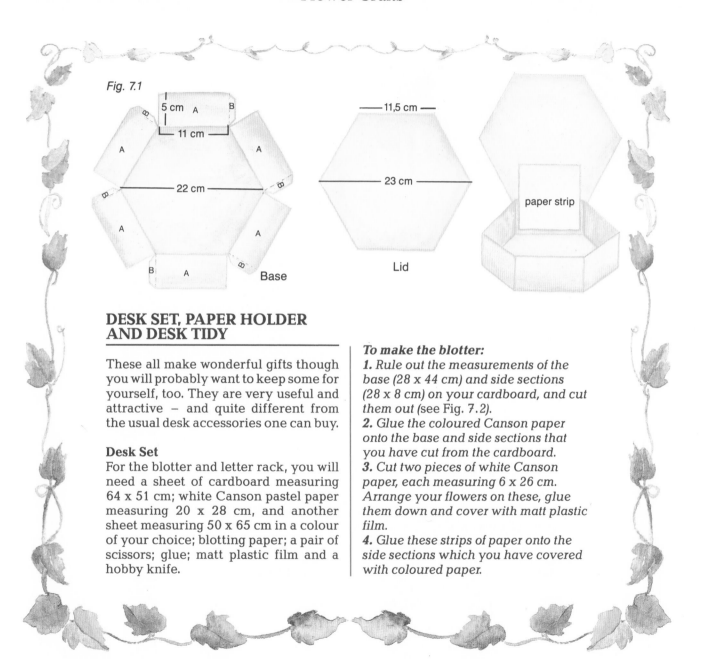

Fig. 7.1

5 cm A B

11 cm

A A

B B

22 cm

B B

A A

B A B

Base

— 11,5 cm —

23 cm

Lid

paper strip

DESK SET, PAPER HOLDER AND DESK TIDY

These all make wonderful gifts though you will probably want to keep some for yourself, too. They are very useful and attractive – and quite different from the usual desk accessories one can buy.

Desk Set

For the blotter and letter rack, you will need a sheet of cardboard measuring 64 x 51 cm; white Canson pastel paper measuring 20 x 28 cm, and another sheet measuring 50 x 65 cm in a colour of your choice; blotting paper; a pair of scissors; glue; matt plastic film and a hobby knife.

To make the blotter:

1. Rule out the measurements of the base (28 x 44 cm) and side sections (28 x 8 cm) on your cardboard, and cut them out (see Fig. 7.2).

2. Glue the coloured Canson paper onto the base and side sections that you have cut from the cardboard.

3. Cut two pieces of white Canson paper, each measuring 6 x 26 cm. Arrange your flowers on these, glue them down and cover with matt plastic film.

4. Glue these strips of paper onto the side sections which you have covered with coloured paper.

5. Run a very narrow line of glue around the three outside edges (marked "A" on the diagram) of each side section and attach them to the base.
6. Cut blotting paper measuring 25,5 x 34 cm and slip it into the blotter.

Fig. 7.2

Side sections

Fig. 7.3

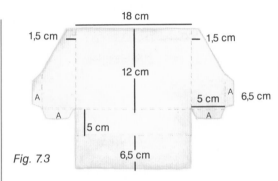

To make the letter rack:
1. Draw out the patterns – beginning with the inner rectangle – using the measurements given in the diagram (see Fig. 7.3). All flaps should be about 1 cm wide. Cut out along the solid lines and score along the dotted lines.
2. Fold along the lines that have been scored and glue the flaps marked "A" to the adjoining sides to form a box shape.
3. Cut the Canson paper to the same pattern, but allow an extra 2 cm along the top and side edges.
4. Glue the coloured paper to the cardboard base, bending the paper carefully at corners. Fold the extending edges

of the coloured paper over the top and glue them down inside.
5. Cut a piece of white paper measuring 5,5 x 16 cm. Arrange the flowers, glue them down and cover with plastic film. Glue this to the front of the rack.

Paper Holder
The paper holder is also made from white cardboard and then covered with attractive paper. You will need a piece of cardboard and coloured paper, each measuring 25 x 15 cm.

1. Draw out the patterns of the box section onto the cardboard following the measurements given in the diagram (see Fig. 7.4). Cut out along the solid lines and score on the dotted lines. Bend along the scored lines to form a box shape. Glue the flaps marked "A" to the adjacent sides.

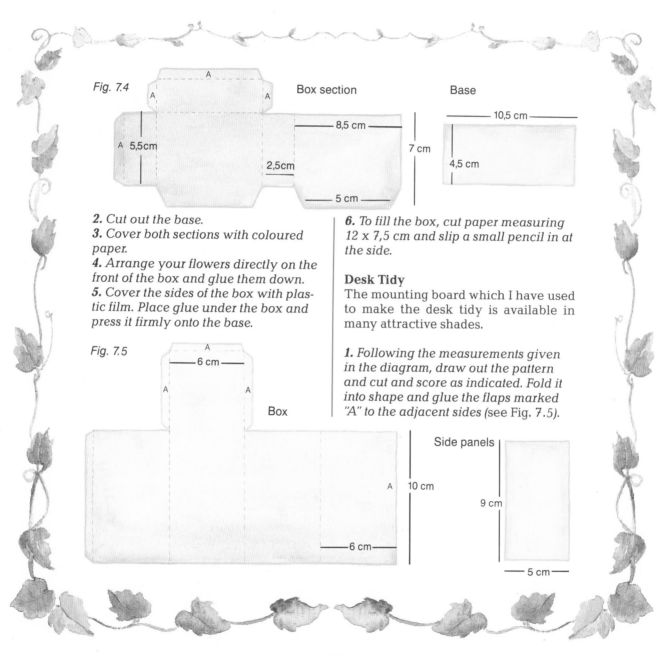

Fig. 7.4   Box section   Base

A

A   A

8,5 cm

A 5,5cm   7 cm

2,5cm   4,5 cm

5 cm   10,5 cm

2. Cut out the base.
3. Cover both sections with coloured paper.
4. Arrange your flowers directly on the front of the box and glue them down.
5. Cover the sides of the box with plastic film. Place glue under the box and press it firmly onto the base.

6. To fill the box, cut paper measuring 12 x 7,5 cm and slip a small pencil in at the side.

Desk Tidy
The mounting board which I have used to make the desk tidy is available in many attractive shades.

1. Following the measurements given in the diagram, draw out the pattern and cut and score as indicated. Fold it into shape and glue the flaps marked "A" to the adjacent sides (see Fig. 7.5).

Fig. 7.5

A

6 cm

A   A

Box

A 10 cm

6 cm

Side panels

9 cm

5 cm

2. Cut four side panels, measuring 9 x 5 cm − as shown in the diagram − and arrange your flower design on them.
3. Glue the plants down and cover each panel with plastic film.
4. Glue the panels to the sides of the box, taking care that the borders are equal.

QUICK PICTURES, COASTERS AND MATS

Quick Pictures

Simple and quick to make, these pictures can give as much pleasure as the more elaborate framed sort. To make them you will need thick cardboard; small pieces of white and coloured paper; matt plastic film; narrow braid; ribbon and a curtain ring.

1. For each picture cut two pieces of cardboard into any shape you want and glue them together. This forms a very strong base which will not bend.
2. Cut a piece of coloured paper the same size as the cardboard and glue it to the base.
3. Measure and cut your white paper into exactly the same shape but make it approximately 1 cm smaller all round.
4. Arrange the flowers on the white paper and glue them down.

5. Glue this to the base and cover the whole picture with plastic film.
6. Carefully glue thin braid around the edges of the entire picture.
7. Fold the ribbon in half, place the curtain ring in the fold and glue the ends of the ribbon onto the back of the picture.
8. Trim the ends of the ribbon.

Coasters and Mats

Pressed flowers can be used to make very pretty coasters and dressing-table mats. Coasters look especially attractive if you make a set with simple, almost botanical designs.

To make these use very strong cardboard and draw out the shapes you require. For each coaster glue two of the shapes together. Cover the cardboard with plain paper in a colour of your choice. Arrange the flowers and glue them down. Cover both the top and bottom with plastic film to protect the coaster from dampness.

I must stress, though, that mats made in this way are not suitable for use as place mats or teapot stands. The heat emanating from the dishes will soon damage the plastic with the result that the flowers will be spoilt by both the heat and moisture.

LAMPSHADES

The best background to use for a lampshade is a fairly stiff parchment, which is available from most good art shops. Alternatively, you can use a good quality paper – providing it is not very dense and will let a fair amount of light glow through it. You will also need matt plastic film; clear glue (for instance Bostik clear); needle and thread, and ribbon or braid.

To begin with I would suggest you buy an inexpensive lampshade with a simple shape. (see Fig. 7.6).

Fig. 7.6

1. Remove the shade carefully from the wire base and use this as the pattern from which to cut your parchment.
2. Arrange your flower design on the parchment and glue the plants down.
3. Cover the whole shade with matt plastic film.

Fig. 7.7

4. Stitch the shade onto the wire frame; overlap the vertical edges and glue them neatly together.
5. Glue ribbon or upholstery trimming around the top and bottom edges to cover the stitching.

A six-sided shade is a bit more difficult to make, but well worth the effort. It is not always possible to buy the correct frame, but many craft or lamp shops will make frames to your specifications.

1. Once you have obtained the frame, mark each panel with a small paper tab – 1, 2, 3, 4, etc. Trace each panel onto the parchment, carefully marking the number of the panel. It is best to do this as no matter how well a frame is made there are always slight variations in the size of the panels.

2. Cut the panels out of the parchment, arrange and glue your flowers down and cover with plastic film.

3. Stitch each panel to the correct section of the frame, over-sewing along the top, bottom and sides (see Fig. 7.7).

4. First glue the ribbon along the side joins and then around the upper and lower edges.

OTHER IDEAS

As you can see from the preceding flower crafts there is endless scope for using your new-found skill. Following the same procedure as you did for cards, you can make attractive bookmarks and stationery. Plain writing paper or notelets will look lovely with a delicate flower design in one of the corners. Bookmarks are perennial favourites but can be rather dull. However, with your pressed flower design they will take on a new dimension.

A photograph album, address book or diary is greatly enhanced if you design a pressed flower picture for the cover. Provided it has a fairly smooth surface you can work directly on the cover and not use any background paper. If, however, the surface is deeply grained or indented you will need to arrange your design on background paper or card and glue this to the book. Protect the flowers with plastic film as before.

If you have a locket, why not make a tiny picture for it? Use flowers which have a very special meaning or memory for you.

With all these new ideas at your fingertips, you will soon find that your birthday and Christmas gift lists present no problem. Added to this will be the joy and satisfaction you will find in your new craft.

A FINAL WORD

In the years I have worked with pressed flowers I have come to appreciate not only the creative rewards, but also enjoy the relaxation and pleasure that this particular art form brings. In this busy, and often jangled, world it becomes increasingly difficult to find such an outlet and I hope that you will find the same enrichment that I have experienced.

Do remember, though, that you are working with nature – and you cannot improve on it, only try to represent it. Simplicity is the keynote, and perhaps that is the whole essence of this craft.